50 Low-Carb Lifestyle Recipes for Home

By: Kelly Johnson

Table of Contents

- Zucchini Noodles with Pesto
- Cauliflower Fried Rice
- Keto Chicken Alfredo
- Eggplant Lasagna
- Avocado Deviled Eggs
- Buffalo Cauliflower Bites
- Almond Flour Pancakes
- Garlic Butter Shrimp
- Broccoli and Cheese Casserole
- Spinach Stuffed Chicken Breast
- Cloud Bread Sandwiches
- Chia Seed Pudding
- Baked Parmesan Zucchini Chips
- Coconut Curry Chicken
- Beef and Broccoli Stir-Fry
- Caprese Salad Skewers
- Mushroom and Swiss Omelette
- Taco Salad with Avocado Dressing
- Creamy Tuscan Garlic Chicken
- Grilled Salmon with Asparagus
- Keto Meatballs with Marinara
- Roasted Brussels Sprouts with Bacon
- Cheesy Cauliflower Bake
- Cabbage Roll Casserole
- Lemon Herb Grilled Chicken
- Greek Salad with Olives and Feta
- Zucchini Fritters
- Coconut Flour Muffins
- Cauliflower Pizza Crust
- Garlic Parmesan Chicken Wings
- Riced Cauliflower Tabbouleh
- Low-Carb Egg Muffins
- Thai Beef Salad
- Egg and Spinach Breakfast Cups
- Shrimp and Avocado Salad
- Pesto Zoodle Salad
- Stuffed Bell Peppers
- Creamy Mushroom Soup
- Coconut Curry Shrimp

- Savory Bacon-Wrapped Asparagus
- Chicken Caesar Salad Lettuce Wraps
- Eggplant Parmesan
- Greek Chicken Skewers
- Taco-Stuffed Avocados
- Spaghetti Squash Bolognese
- Baked Lemon Herb Tilapia
- Sausage and Pepper Skillet
- Cinnamon Cream Cheese Roll-Ups
- Cilantro Lime Cauliflower Rice
- Chocolate Avocado Mousse

Zucchini Noodles with Pesto

Ingredients:

- **For the Zoodles:**
    - 2 medium zucchinis
    - 1 tablespoon olive oil
    - Salt and pepper to taste
- **For the Pesto:**
    - 2 cups fresh basil leaves
    - 1/3 cup pine nuts (or walnuts)
    - 1/2 cup grated Parmesan cheese
    - 2-3 garlic cloves
    - 1/2 cup olive oil
    - Salt and pepper to taste
- **Optional toppings:**
    - Cherry tomatoes, halved
    - Extra Parmesan cheese
    - Crushed red pepper flakes

Instructions:

1. Using a spiralizer or vegetable peeler, create zucchini noodles from the zucchinis.
2. Heat olive oil in a skillet over medium heat. Add zoodles and sauté for 2-3 minutes until just tender. Season with salt and pepper. Set aside.
3. In a food processor, combine basil leaves, pine nuts, Parmesan cheese, and garlic. Pulse until finely chopped.
4. With the processor running, slowly drizzle in olive oil until smooth. Season with salt and pepper.
5. In the skillet with zoodles, add pesto and toss until well coated. Add a splash of pasta cooking water or more olive oil if too thick.
6. Serve topped with cherry tomatoes and extra Parmesan, if desired.

Cauliflower Fried Rice

Ingredients:

- 1 medium head of cauliflower, riced
- 2 tablespoons sesame oil (or olive oil)
- 2 eggs, beaten
- 1 cup mixed vegetables (carrots, peas, bell peppers)
- 3 green onions, sliced
- 2-3 cloves garlic, minced
- 2-3 tablespoons soy sauce (or tamari for gluten-free)
- Salt and pepper to taste

Instructions:

1. Rice the cauliflower using a food processor or grater.
2. Heat sesame oil in a large skillet or wok over medium heat. Add the garlic and sauté for 30 seconds.
3. Push the garlic to the side and pour in the beaten eggs, scrambling them until fully cooked.
4. Add mixed vegetables and sauté for 2-3 minutes until tender.
5. Stir in the riced cauliflower and soy sauce. Cook for another 5-7 minutes, stirring occasionally. Season with salt and pepper.
6. Stir in green onions before serving.

Enjoy both recipes for a delicious, healthy meal!

Keto Chicken Alfredo

Ingredients:

- 2 chicken breasts, cooked and sliced
- 1 cup heavy cream
- 1 cup grated Parmesan cheese
- 2 tablespoons butter
- 2 garlic cloves, minced
- Salt and pepper to taste
- Fresh parsley for garnish

Instructions:

1. In a skillet, melt butter over medium heat. Add garlic and sauté for 1 minute.
2. Pour in heavy cream and simmer for 5 minutes.
3. Stir in Parmesan cheese until melted and smooth. Season with salt and pepper.
4. Add sliced chicken and cook until heated through.
5. Serve garnished with parsley.

Eggplant Lasagna

Ingredients:

- 2 large eggplants, sliced lengthwise
- 2 cups marinara sauce (sugar-free)
- 2 cups ricotta cheese
- 2 cups shredded mozzarella cheese
- 1/2 cup grated Parmesan cheese
- 1 teaspoon Italian seasoning
- Salt and pepper to taste

Instructions:

1. Preheat oven to 375°F (190°C).
2. Salt the eggplant slices and let sit for 20 minutes to draw out moisture. Rinse and pat dry.
3. Layer eggplant slices, ricotta, marinara, mozzarella, and Parmesan in a baking dish. Repeat layers, finishing with mozzarella on top.
4. Bake for 30-35 minutes until bubbly and golden. Let cool before slicing.

Avocado Deviled Eggs

Ingredients:

- 6 hard-boiled eggs
- 1 ripe avocado
- 1 tablespoon lime juice
- 1 teaspoon Dijon mustard
- Salt and pepper to taste
- Paprika for garnish

Instructions:

1. Slice hard-boiled eggs in half and remove yolks.
2. In a bowl, mash yolks with avocado, lime juice, mustard, salt, and pepper until smooth.
3. Fill egg whites with the avocado mixture. Sprinkle with paprika before serving.

Buffalo Cauliflower Bites

Ingredients:

- 1 head of cauliflower, cut into florets
- 1/2 cup almond flour
- 1/2 cup water
- 1/2 cup buffalo sauce
- 1 tablespoon olive oil

Instructions:

1. Preheat oven to 450°F (230°C).
2. In a bowl, mix almond flour with water to create a batter.
3. Dip cauliflower florets into the batter, then place on a baking sheet. Bake for 20 minutes.
4. Toss baked cauliflower in buffalo sauce and return to the oven for another 10 minutes.

Almond Flour Pancakes

Ingredients:

- 1 cup almond flour
- 2 eggs
- 1/4 cup unsweetened almond milk
- 1 teaspoon baking powder
- 1 teaspoon vanilla extract
- Butter or oil for cooking

Instructions:

1. In a bowl, mix almond flour, eggs, almond milk, baking powder, and vanilla until smooth.
2. Heat butter or oil in a skillet over medium heat. Pour batter to form pancakes. Cook until bubbles form, then flip and cook until golden.
3. Serve with sugar-free syrup or berries.

Garlic Butter Shrimp

Ingredients:

- 1 pound shrimp, peeled and deveined
- 4 tablespoons butter
- 4 garlic cloves, minced
- 1 tablespoon lemon juice
- Salt and pepper to taste
- Fresh parsley for garnish

Instructions:

1. In a skillet, melt butter over medium heat. Add garlic and sauté for 1 minute.
2. Add shrimp, season with salt and pepper, and cook until pink (about 3-4 minutes).
3. Stir in lemon juice and garnish with parsley before serving.

Broccoli and Cheese Casserole

Ingredients:

- 4 cups broccoli florets (fresh or frozen)
- 2 cups shredded cheddar cheese
- 1 cup heavy cream
- 1/2 cup cream cheese, softened
- 1 teaspoon garlic powder
- Salt and pepper to taste

Instructions:

1. Preheat oven to 350°F (175°C).
2. In a large bowl, combine broccoli, cheddar cheese, heavy cream, cream cheese, garlic powder, salt, and pepper.
3. Transfer to a greased baking dish and bake for 25-30 minutes until bubbly and golden.

Spinach Stuffed Chicken Breast

Ingredients:

- 2 chicken breasts
- 1 cup fresh spinach, cooked and chopped
- 1/2 cup cream cheese, softened
- 1/4 cup grated Parmesan cheese
- 1 teaspoon garlic powder
- Salt and pepper to taste

Instructions:

1. Preheat oven to 375°F (190°C).
2. Mix spinach, cream cheese, Parmesan, garlic powder, salt, and pepper in a bowl.
3. Cut a pocket in each chicken breast and fill with the spinach mixture.
4. Bake for 25-30 minutes until chicken is cooked through.

Enjoy these delicious keto-friendly recipes!

Cloud Bread Sandwiches

Ingredients:

- 3 large eggs
- 3 ounces cream cheese, softened
- 1/4 teaspoon cream of tartar
- Pinch of salt

Instructions:

1. Preheat oven to 300°F (150°C).
2. In a bowl, beat egg whites with cream of tartar until stiff peaks form.
3. In another bowl, mix egg yolks, cream cheese, and salt until smooth.
4. Gently fold egg whites into the yolk mixture.
5. Drop spoonfuls onto a parchment-lined baking sheet and shape into rounds.
6. Bake for 25-30 minutes until golden. Use as sandwich bread.

Chia Seed Pudding

Ingredients:

- 1/4 cup chia seeds
- 1 cup unsweetened almond milk
- 1 tablespoon maple syrup or sweetener of choice
- 1/2 teaspoon vanilla extract

Instructions:

1. In a bowl, combine chia seeds, almond milk, maple syrup, and vanilla.
2. Stir well and let sit for 10 minutes. Stir again to prevent clumping.
3. Cover and refrigerate for at least 2 hours or overnight. Serve chilled with toppings like berries or nuts.

Baked Parmesan Zucchini Chips

Ingredients:

- 2 medium zucchinis, thinly sliced
- 1 cup grated Parmesan cheese
- 1 teaspoon garlic powder
- Salt and pepper to taste

Instructions:

1. Preheat oven to 225°F (110°C).
2. Toss zucchini slices with garlic powder, salt, and pepper.
3. Arrange on a baking sheet and sprinkle with Parmesan.
4. Bake for 1-2 hours until crispy, flipping halfway through.

Coconut Curry Chicken

Ingredients:

- 1 pound chicken breast, diced
- 1 can (13.5 oz) coconut milk
- 2 tablespoons curry powder
- 1 onion, diced
- 2 garlic cloves, minced
- Salt to taste
- Fresh cilantro for garnish

Instructions:

1. In a skillet, sauté onion and garlic until soft.
2. Add chicken and cook until browned.
3. Stir in coconut milk and curry powder. Simmer for 15-20 minutes.
4. Season with salt and garnish with cilantro before serving.

Beef and Broccoli Stir-Fry

Ingredients:

- 1 pound beef (sirloin or flank), thinly sliced
- 2 cups broccoli florets
- 2 tablespoons soy sauce
- 1 tablespoon sesame oil
- 2 garlic cloves, minced
- 1 teaspoon ginger, minced

Instructions:

1. Heat sesame oil in a skillet over medium-high heat.
2. Add garlic and ginger, sautéing for 30 seconds.
3. Add beef and cook until browned.
4. Stir in broccoli and soy sauce; cook for another 5 minutes until broccoli is tender.

Caprese Salad Skewers

Ingredients:

- Cherry tomatoes
- Fresh mozzarella balls
- Fresh basil leaves
- Balsamic glaze for drizzling
- Salt and pepper to taste

Instructions:

1. On skewers, alternate cherry tomatoes, mozzarella, and basil.
2. Drizzle with balsamic glaze and season with salt and pepper before serving.

Mushroom and Swiss Omelette

Ingredients:

- 3 large eggs
- 1 cup mushrooms, sliced
- 1/2 cup shredded Swiss cheese
- 1 tablespoon butter
- Salt and pepper to taste

Instructions:

1. In a skillet, melt butter and sauté mushrooms until soft.
2. In a bowl, whisk eggs with salt and pepper.
3. Pour eggs into the skillet and cook until edges set.
4. Add cheese and mushrooms, fold omelette, and cook until cheese melts.

Taco Salad with Avocado Dressing

Ingredients:

- 1 pound ground beef or turkey
- 1 tablespoon taco seasoning
- 4 cups lettuce, chopped
- 1 cup cherry tomatoes, halved
- 1 avocado
- 2 tablespoons lime juice
- Salt and pepper to taste

Instructions:

1. In a skillet, cook ground meat with taco seasoning until browned.
2. In a blender, combine avocado, lime juice, salt, and pepper; blend until smooth.
3. In a bowl, layer lettuce, tomatoes, and meat. Drizzle with avocado dressing before serving.

Enjoy these delicious and healthy recipes!

Creamy Tuscan Garlic Chicken

Ingredients:

- 2 chicken breasts
- 1 tablespoon olive oil
- 3 garlic cloves, minced
- 1 cup heavy cream
- 1 cup spinach, chopped
- 1/2 cup sun-dried tomatoes, chopped
- 1/2 cup grated Parmesan cheese
- Salt and pepper to taste
- Fresh basil for garnish

Instructions:

1. In a skillet, heat olive oil over medium heat. Season chicken breasts with salt and pepper, then cook until golden and cooked through. Remove and set aside.
2. In the same skillet, add garlic and sauté for 1 minute.
3. Stir in heavy cream, sun-dried tomatoes, and spinach. Simmer for 5 minutes until slightly thickened.
4. Add Parmesan cheese and stir until melted. Return chicken to the skillet, coating it in the sauce. Garnish with fresh basil before serving.

Grilled Salmon with Asparagus

Ingredients:

- 2 salmon fillets
- 1 bunch asparagus, trimmed
- 2 tablespoons olive oil
- 1 lemon, sliced
- Salt and pepper to taste

Instructions:

1. Preheat grill to medium-high heat.
2. Drizzle salmon and asparagus with olive oil; season with salt and pepper.
3. Place salmon and asparagus on the grill. Cook salmon for about 4-5 minutes per side and asparagus for about 3-4 minutes until tender.
4. Serve with lemon slices.

Keto Meatballs with Marinara

Ingredients:

- 1 pound ground beef or turkey
- 1/4 cup almond flour
- 1 egg
- 2 cloves garlic, minced
- 1 teaspoon Italian seasoning
- 1 jar (24 oz) sugar-free marinara sauce

Instructions:

1. Preheat oven to 400°F (200°C).
2. In a bowl, combine meat, almond flour, egg, garlic, Italian seasoning, salt, and pepper. Mix until combined.
3. Form into meatballs and place on a baking sheet. Bake for 20-25 minutes until cooked through.
4. Heat marinara sauce in a saucepan, then add meatballs and simmer for 5 minutes before serving.

Roasted Brussels Sprouts with Bacon

Ingredients:

- 1 pound Brussels sprouts, halved
- 4 strips bacon, chopped
- 2 tablespoons olive oil
- Salt and pepper to taste

Instructions:

1. Preheat oven to 400°F (200°C).
2. Toss Brussels sprouts and bacon in a bowl with olive oil, salt, and pepper.
3. Spread on a baking sheet and roast for 20-25 minutes until crispy and golden.

Cheesy Cauliflower Bake

Ingredients:

- 1 head cauliflower, cut into florets
- 1 cup shredded cheddar cheese
- 1/2 cup cream cheese, softened
- 1/4 cup heavy cream
- 1 teaspoon garlic powder
- Salt and pepper to taste

Instructions:

1. Preheat oven to 350°F (175°C).
2. Steam cauliflower until tender, about 5-7 minutes.
3. In a bowl, mix cream cheese, heavy cream, garlic powder, salt, and pepper. Stir in cauliflower and half the cheddar cheese.
4. Transfer to a baking dish, top with remaining cheese, and bake for 20-25 minutes until bubbly.

Cabbage Roll Casserole

Ingredients:

- 1 pound ground beef
- 1 onion, diced
- 1 head green cabbage, chopped
- 1 can (14 oz) diced tomatoes
- 2 cups tomato sauce
- 1 teaspoon Italian seasoning
- Salt and pepper to taste

Instructions:

1. Preheat oven to 375°F (190°C).
2. In a skillet, cook ground beef and onion until browned.
3. In a large bowl, mix cabbage, tomatoes, tomato sauce, Italian seasoning, salt, and pepper.
4. Combine with the beef mixture, transfer to a baking dish, and bake for 30-40 minutes until cabbage is tender.

Lemon Herb Grilled Chicken

Ingredients:

- 2 chicken breasts
- 1/4 cup olive oil
- 2 tablespoons lemon juice
- 2 teaspoons dried oregano
- 2 teaspoons garlic powder
- Salt and pepper to taste

Instructions:

1. In a bowl, whisk together olive oil, lemon juice, oregano, garlic powder, salt, and pepper.
2. Marinate chicken in the mixture for at least 30 minutes.
3. Preheat grill to medium-high heat and cook chicken for 6-7 minutes per side until cooked through.

Greek Salad with Olives and Feta

Ingredients:

- 2 cups cucumbers, diced
- 1 cup cherry tomatoes, halved
- 1/2 cup red onion, thinly sliced
- 1/2 cup Kalamata olives
- 1/2 cup feta cheese, crumbled
- 2 tablespoons olive oil
- 1 tablespoon red wine vinegar
- Salt and pepper to taste

Instructions:

1. In a large bowl, combine cucumbers, tomatoes, onion, olives, and feta.
2. Drizzle with olive oil and red wine vinegar; season with salt and pepper.
3. Toss gently and serve chilled.

Enjoy these delicious meals!

Creamy Tuscan Garlic Chicken

Ingredients:

- 2 chicken breasts
- 1 tablespoon olive oil
- 3 garlic cloves, minced
- 1 cup heavy cream
- 1 cup spinach, chopped
- 1/2 cup sun-dried tomatoes, chopped
- 1/2 cup grated Parmesan cheese
- Salt and pepper to taste
- Fresh basil for garnish

Instructions:

1. In a skillet, heat olive oil over medium heat. Season chicken with salt and pepper, then cook until golden and cooked through. Remove and set aside.
2. In the same skillet, add garlic and sauté for 1 minute.
3. Stir in heavy cream, sun-dried tomatoes, and spinach. Simmer for 5 minutes until slightly thickened.
4. Add Parmesan cheese and stir until melted. Return chicken to the skillet, coating it in the sauce. Garnish with fresh basil before serving.

Grilled Salmon with Asparagus

Ingredients:

- 2 salmon fillets
- 1 bunch asparagus, trimmed
- 2 tablespoons olive oil
- 1 lemon, sliced
- Salt and pepper to taste

Instructions:

1. Preheat grill to medium-high heat.
2. Drizzle salmon and asparagus with olive oil; season with salt and pepper.
3. Place salmon and asparagus on the grill. Cook salmon for about 4-5 minutes per side and asparagus for about 3-4 minutes until tender.
4. Serve with lemon slices.

Keto Meatballs with Marinara

Ingredients:

- 1 pound ground beef or turkey
- 1/4 cup almond flour
- 1 egg
- 2 cloves garlic, minced
- 1 teaspoon Italian seasoning
- 1 jar (24 oz) sugar-free marinara sauce

Instructions:

1. Preheat oven to 400°F (200°C).
2. In a bowl, combine meat, almond flour, egg, garlic, Italian seasoning, salt, and pepper. Mix until combined.
3. Form into meatballs and place on a baking sheet. Bake for 20-25 minutes until cooked through.
4. Heat marinara sauce in a saucepan, then add meatballs and simmer for 5 minutes before serving.

Roasted Brussels Sprouts with Bacon

Ingredients:

- 1 pound Brussels sprouts, halved
- 4 strips bacon, chopped
- 2 tablespoons olive oil
- Salt and pepper to taste

Instructions:

1. Preheat oven to 400°F (200°C).
2. Toss Brussels sprouts and bacon in a bowl with olive oil, salt, and pepper.
3. Spread on a baking sheet and roast for 20-25 minutes until crispy and golden.

Cheesy Cauliflower Bake

Ingredients:

- 1 head cauliflower, cut into florets
- 1 cup shredded cheddar cheese
- 1/2 cup cream cheese, softened
- 1/4 cup heavy cream
- 1 teaspoon garlic powder
- Salt and pepper to taste

Instructions:

1. Preheat oven to 350°F (175°C).
2. Steam cauliflower until tender, about 5-7 minutes.
3. In a bowl, mix cream cheese, heavy cream, garlic powder, salt, and pepper. Stir in cauliflower and half the cheddar cheese.
4. Transfer to a baking dish, top with remaining cheese, and bake for 20-25 minutes until bubbly.

Cabbage Roll Casserole

Ingredients:

- 1 pound ground beef
- 1 onion, diced
- 1 head green cabbage, chopped
- 1 can (14 oz) diced tomatoes
- 2 cups tomato sauce
- 1 teaspoon Italian seasoning
- Salt and pepper to taste

Instructions:

1. Preheat oven to 375°F (190°C).
2. In a skillet, cook ground beef and onion until browned.
3. In a large bowl, mix cabbage, tomatoes, tomato sauce, Italian seasoning, salt, and pepper.
4. Combine with the beef mixture, transfer to a baking dish, and bake for 30-40 minutes until cabbage is tender.

Lemon Herb Grilled Chicken

Ingredients:

- 2 chicken breasts
- 1/4 cup olive oil
- 2 tablespoons lemon juice
- 2 teaspoons dried oregano
- 2 teaspoons garlic powder
- Salt and pepper to taste

Instructions:

1. In a bowl, whisk together olive oil, lemon juice, oregano, garlic powder, salt, and pepper.
2. Marinate chicken in the mixture for at least 30 minutes.
3. Preheat grill to medium-high heat and cook chicken for 6-7 minutes per side until cooked through.

Greek Salad with Olives and Feta

Ingredients:

- 2 cups cucumbers, diced
- 1 cup cherry tomatoes, halved
- 1/2 cup red onion, thinly sliced
- 1/2 cup Kalamata olives
- 1/2 cup feta cheese, crumbled
- 2 tablespoons olive oil
- 1 tablespoon red wine vinegar
- Salt and pepper to taste

Instructions:

1. In a large bowl, combine cucumbers, tomatoes, onion, olives, and feta.
2. Drizzle with olive oil and red wine vinegar; season with salt and pepper.
3. Toss gently and serve chilled.

Enjoy your delicious meals!

Zucchini Fritters

Ingredients:

- 2 medium zucchinis, grated
- 1/2 cup almond flour
- 1/4 cup grated Parmesan cheese
- 2 eggs, beaten
- 2 green onions, chopped
- 2 cloves garlic, minced
- Salt and pepper to taste
- Olive oil for frying

Instructions:

1. Squeeze excess moisture from grated zucchini using a kitchen towel.
2. In a bowl, combine zucchini, almond flour, Parmesan, eggs, green onions, garlic, salt, and pepper.
3. Heat olive oil in a skillet over medium heat.
4. Drop spoonfuls of the mixture into the skillet, flattening slightly. Cook until golden brown on both sides, about 3-4 minutes per side.
5. Drain on paper towels and serve warm.

Coconut Flour Muffins

Ingredients:

- 1/2 cup coconut flour
- 1/2 teaspoon baking powder
- 1/4 teaspoon salt
- 4 eggs
- 1/4 cup coconut oil, melted
- 1/4 cup honey or sweetener of choice
- 1 teaspoon vanilla extract

Instructions:

1. Preheat oven to 350°F (175°C) and line a muffin tin with paper liners.
2. In a bowl, mix coconut flour, baking powder, and salt.
3. In another bowl, whisk eggs, then add melted coconut oil, honey, and vanilla.
4. Combine wet and dry ingredients until smooth.
5. Fill muffin cups and bake for 15-20 minutes until golden and a toothpick comes out clean.

Cauliflower Pizza Crust

Ingredients:

- 1 head cauliflower, riced
- 1 cup shredded mozzarella cheese
- 1/4 cup grated Parmesan cheese
- 2 eggs
- 1 teaspoon Italian seasoning
- Salt and pepper to taste

Instructions:

1. Preheat oven to 425°F (220°C) and line a baking sheet with parchment paper.
2. Steam cauliflower rice until tender, then let cool and squeeze out excess moisture.
3. In a bowl, mix cauliflower, mozzarella, Parmesan, eggs, Italian seasoning, salt, and pepper.
4. Spread the mixture into a pizza shape on the baking sheet.
5. Bake for 15-20 minutes until golden, then add toppings and bake again until melted.

Garlic Parmesan Chicken Wings

Ingredients:

- 2 pounds chicken wings
- 1/4 cup melted butter
- 4 cloves garlic, minced
- 1/2 cup grated Parmesan cheese
- 1 teaspoon garlic powder
- Salt and pepper to taste

Instructions:

1. Preheat oven to 400°F (200°C).
2. In a bowl, combine melted butter, garlic, Parmesan, garlic powder, salt, and pepper.
3. Toss chicken wings in the mixture until well coated.
4. Place wings on a baking sheet and bake for 40-45 minutes until crispy and golden, flipping halfway through.

Riced Cauliflower Tabbouleh

Ingredients:

- 1 head cauliflower, riced
- 1 cup cherry tomatoes, diced
- 1 cucumber, diced
- 1/4 cup parsley, chopped
- 1/4 cup green onions, chopped
- 3 tablespoons olive oil
- 2 tablespoons lemon juice
- Salt and pepper to taste

Instructions:

1. In a large bowl, combine riced cauliflower, tomatoes, cucumber, parsley, and green onions.
2. Drizzle with olive oil and lemon juice; season with salt and pepper.
3. Toss well and serve chilled.

Low-Carb Egg Muffins

Ingredients:

- 6 large eggs
- 1/2 cup bell peppers, diced
- 1/2 cup spinach, chopped
- 1/4 cup cheese (cheddar or your choice)
- Salt and pepper to taste

Instructions:

1. Preheat oven to 350°F (175°C) and grease a muffin tin.
2. In a bowl, whisk eggs, then add bell peppers, spinach, cheese, salt, and pepper.
3. Pour the mixture into muffin cups, filling about 2/3 full.
4. Bake for 15-20 minutes until set and lightly golden.

Thai Beef Salad

Ingredients:

- 1 pound beef (flank steak or sirloin), grilled and sliced
- 4 cups mixed greens
- 1 cucumber, sliced
- 1 red bell pepper, sliced
- 1/4 cup fresh cilantro, chopped
- 1/4 cup lime juice
- 2 tablespoons fish sauce
- 1 tablespoon honey or sweetener
- 1 teaspoon chili flakes

Instructions:

1. In a large bowl, combine mixed greens, cucumber, bell pepper, and cilantro.
2. In a separate bowl, whisk together lime juice, fish sauce, honey, and chili flakes.
3. Add sliced beef to the salad and drizzle with dressing. Toss well and serve.

Egg and Spinach Breakfast Cups

Ingredients:

- 6 large eggs
- 1 cup fresh spinach, chopped
- 1/2 cup diced tomatoes
- 1/4 cup feta cheese (optional)
- Salt and pepper to taste

Instructions:

1. Preheat oven to 350°F (175°C) and grease a muffin tin.
2. In a bowl, whisk eggs and season with salt and pepper.
3. Stir in spinach, tomatoes, and feta.
4. Pour the mixture into muffin cups, filling about 2/3 full.
5. Bake for 15-20 minutes until set and lightly golden.

Enjoy your delicious meals!

Shrimp and Avocado Salad

Ingredients:

- 1 pound shrimp, peeled and deveined
- 1 avocado, diced
- 1 cup cherry tomatoes, halved
- 1/4 cup red onion, diced
- 2 tablespoons olive oil
- 1 tablespoon lime juice
- Salt and pepper to taste
- Fresh cilantro for garnish

Instructions:

1. In a skillet, heat olive oil over medium heat. Cook shrimp until pink and cooked through, about 3-4 minutes.
2. In a large bowl, combine shrimp, avocado, tomatoes, onion, lime juice, salt, and pepper.
3. Toss gently and garnish with cilantro before serving.

Pesto Zoodle Salad

Ingredients:

- 2 medium zucchinis, spiralized
- 1 cup cherry tomatoes, halved
- 1/4 cup basil pesto
- 1/4 cup grated Parmesan cheese
- Salt and pepper to taste

Instructions:

1. In a large bowl, combine spiralized zucchini, tomatoes, pesto, and Parmesan.
2. Toss until well mixed and season with salt and pepper.
3. Serve immediately or chill for 30 minutes before serving.

Stuffed Bell Peppers

Ingredients:

- 4 bell peppers, tops cut off and seeds removed
- 1 pound ground turkey or beef
- 1 cup cauliflower rice
- 1 can (14 oz) diced tomatoes
- 1 teaspoon Italian seasoning
- Salt and pepper to taste
- 1 cup shredded cheese (optional)

Instructions:

1. Preheat oven to 375°F (190°C).
2. In a skillet, cook ground meat until browned. Add cauliflower rice, diced tomatoes, Italian seasoning, salt, and pepper.
3. Stuff the mixture into the bell peppers and place in a baking dish.
4. If using cheese, sprinkle on top. Bake for 30-35 minutes until peppers are tender.

Creamy Mushroom Soup

Ingredients:

- 1 pound mushrooms, sliced
- 1 onion, diced
- 3 garlic cloves, minced
- 4 cups vegetable or chicken broth
- 1 cup heavy cream
- 2 tablespoons olive oil
- Salt and pepper to taste
- Fresh thyme for garnish

Instructions:

1. In a pot, heat olive oil over medium heat. Sauté onion and garlic until soft.
2. Add mushrooms and cook until browned.
3. Pour in broth and bring to a boil. Simmer for 15 minutes.
4. Blend until smooth, then stir in heavy cream. Season with salt and pepper. Garnish with thyme before serving.

Coconut Curry Shrimp

Ingredients:

- 1 pound shrimp, peeled and deveined
- 1 can (13.5 oz) coconut milk
- 2 tablespoons red curry paste
- 1 tablespoon fish sauce
- 1 tablespoon lime juice
- 1 cup bell peppers, sliced
- Fresh cilantro for garnish

Instructions:

1. In a skillet, heat coconut milk and red curry paste over medium heat until combined.
2. Add shrimp and bell peppers; cook until shrimp is pink and cooked through, about 5 minutes.
3. Stir in fish sauce and lime juice. Garnish with cilantro before serving.

Savory Bacon-Wrapped Asparagus

Ingredients:

- 1 bunch asparagus, trimmed
- 8 strips of bacon
- Olive oil
- Salt and pepper to taste

Instructions:

1. Preheat oven to 400°F (200°C).
2. Wrap each asparagus spear with a strip of bacon.
3. Place on a baking sheet, drizzle with olive oil, and season with salt and pepper.
4. Bake for 15-20 minutes until bacon is crispy.

Chicken Caesar Salad Lettuce Wraps

Ingredients:

- 2 cups cooked chicken, diced
- 1/2 cup Caesar dressing
- 1/4 cup grated Parmesan cheese
- Romaine lettuce leaves
- Croutons (optional)

Instructions:

1. In a bowl, combine chicken, Caesar dressing, and Parmesan.
2. Spoon the mixture into romaine leaves.
3. Top with croutons if desired and serve immediately.

Eggplant Parmesan

Ingredients:

- 2 medium eggplants, sliced
- 2 cups marinara sauce
- 2 cups shredded mozzarella cheese
- 1/2 cup grated Parmesan cheese
- 1 teaspoon Italian seasoning
- Olive oil for brushing
- Salt and pepper to taste

Instructions:

1. Preheat oven to 375°F (190°C).
2. Salt the eggplant slices and let sit for 30 minutes to draw out moisture. Rinse and pat dry.
3. Brush eggplant with olive oil and roast in the oven for 20 minutes until tender.
4. In a baking dish, layer marinara sauce, eggplant, mozzarella, and Parmesan. Repeat layers, finishing with cheese.
5. Bake for 30-35 minutes until bubbly and golden.

Enjoy these flavorful dishes!

Greek Chicken Skewers

Ingredients:

- 1 pound chicken breast, cubed
- 1/4 cup olive oil
- 2 tablespoons lemon juice
- 2 teaspoons dried oregano
- 2 cloves garlic, minced
- Salt and pepper to taste
- Wooden skewers, soaked in water

Instructions:

1. In a bowl, whisk together olive oil, lemon juice, oregano, garlic, salt, and pepper.
2. Add chicken to the marinade and let it sit for at least 30 minutes.
3. Preheat grill to medium-high heat.
4. Thread chicken onto skewers and grill for 10-12 minutes, turning occasionally, until cooked through. Serve with tzatziki sauce.

Taco-Stuffed Avocados

Ingredients:

- 2 ripe avocados, halved and pitted
- 1 pound ground beef or turkey
- 1 packet taco seasoning
- 1 cup cherry tomatoes, diced
- 1/2 cup shredded cheese (cheddar or Mexican blend)
- Sour cream and cilantro for topping

Instructions:

1. In a skillet, cook ground meat until browned, then add taco seasoning and water according to package instructions.
2. Fill each avocado half with the taco meat mixture.
3. Top with diced tomatoes, cheese, sour cream, and cilantro before serving.

Spaghetti Squash Bolognese

Ingredients:

- 1 medium spaghetti squash
- 1 pound ground beef or turkey
- 1 onion, diced
- 2 cloves garlic, minced
- 1 can (14 oz) crushed tomatoes
- 1 teaspoon Italian seasoning
- Salt and pepper to taste
- Fresh basil for garnish

Instructions:

1. Preheat oven to 400°F (200°C). Cut spaghetti squash in half, remove seeds, and place cut-side down on a baking sheet. Bake for 30-40 minutes until tender.
2. In a skillet, cook onion and garlic until soft. Add ground meat and cook until browned.
3. Stir in crushed tomatoes, Italian seasoning, salt, and pepper; simmer for 10 minutes.
4. Scrape the spaghetti squash with a fork to create strands and serve topped with the Bolognese sauce and fresh basil.

Baked Lemon Herb Tilapia

Ingredients:

- 4 tilapia fillets
- 2 tablespoons olive oil
- 2 tablespoons lemon juice
- 1 teaspoon dried thyme
- 1 teaspoon garlic powder
- Salt and pepper to taste
- Lemon slices for garnish

Instructions:

1. Preheat oven to 375°F (190°C).
2. In a baking dish, arrange tilapia fillets. Drizzle with olive oil and lemon juice, then sprinkle with thyme, garlic powder, salt, and pepper.
3. Bake for 15-20 minutes until fish flakes easily with a fork. Garnish with lemon slices before serving.

Sausage and Pepper Skillet

Ingredients:

- 1 pound Italian sausage, sliced
- 1 bell pepper, sliced
- 1 onion, sliced
- 2 cloves garlic, minced
- 1 can (14 oz) diced tomatoes
- Salt and pepper to taste
- Fresh parsley for garnish

Instructions:

1. In a skillet, cook sausage over medium heat until browned.
2. Add bell pepper, onion, and garlic; sauté until vegetables are tender.
3. Stir in diced tomatoes, salt, and pepper; simmer for 10 minutes. Garnish with parsley before serving.

Cinnamon Cream Cheese Roll-Ups

Ingredients:

- 4 low-carb tortillas
- 8 oz cream cheese, softened
- 1/4 cup sweetener (like erythritol)
- 1 teaspoon cinnamon
- 1 tablespoon butter

Instructions:

1. In a bowl, mix cream cheese, sweetener, and cinnamon until smooth.
2. Spread the mixture evenly over each tortilla and roll them up tightly.
3. In a skillet, melt butter over medium heat and cook the roll-ups until golden on all sides. Slice and serve warm.

Cilantro Lime Cauliflower Rice

Ingredients:

- 1 head cauliflower, riced
- 2 tablespoons olive oil
- 1 lime, juiced
- 1/4 cup fresh cilantro, chopped
- Salt to taste

Instructions:

1. In a skillet, heat olive oil over medium heat. Add riced cauliflower and sauté for about 5 minutes until tender.
2. Stir in lime juice, cilantro, and salt. Cook for an additional minute and serve.

Chocolate Avocado Mousse

Ingredients:

- 2 ripe avocados
- 1/4 cup unsweetened cocoa powder
- 1/4 cup sweetener (like maple syrup or agave)
- 1/4 cup almond milk
- 1 teaspoon vanilla extract

Instructions:

1. In a blender, combine avocados, cocoa powder, sweetener, almond milk, and vanilla. Blend until smooth and creamy.
2. Adjust sweetness if needed and refrigerate for at least 30 minutes before serving.

Enjoy these delicious and healthy recipes!

www.ingramcontent.com/pod-product-compliance
Lightning Source LLC
LaVergne TN
LVHW081319060526
838201LV00055B/2372